Weatherwise

Rain and Floods

Patience Coster

PowerKiDS
press

New York

Published in 2010 by The Rosen Publishing Group Inc.
29 East 21st Street, New York, NY 10010

Copyright © 2010 Wayland/
The Rosen Publishing Group, Inc.

First Edition

Design: Rob Norridge and Paul Myerscough
Editor: Sarah Eason
Editor for Wayland: Claire Shanahan
Illustrations: Geoff Ward
Photography by Tudor Photography
Picture research: Maria Joannou
Consultant: Harold Pratt

Library of Congress Cataloging-in-Publication Data

Coster, Patience.
Rain and floods / Patience Coster.
p. cm. – (Weatherwise)
Includes index.
ISBN 978-1-61532-261-9 (library binding)
ISBN 978-1-61532-274-9 (paperback)
ISBN 978-1-61532-275-6 (6-pack)
1. Rain and rainfall–Juvenile literature. 2. Floods–Juvenile literature. I. Title.
QC924.7.C67 2010
551.57'7–dc22
2009026801

Photographs:
Alamy Images: Andrew Fox 11; Corbis: Ashley Cooper 26, Gideon Mendel 1, 19, Reuters/Utpal
Baruah 23, Reuters/Richard Chung 6; Fotolia: J-F Perigois 24; Getty Images: Deshakalyan
Chowdhury/AFP 22, Marko Georgiev 21; Shutterstock: Galyna Andrushko 9, Anyka 12,
Magdalena Bujak 17, Tony Campbell 20, Four Oaks 18, Bartosz Hadyniak 14,
Craig Hanson 16, Eric Isselée 5, Luciano Mortula 25, Nic Neish 13, PhotoSmart 4,
Dr. Morley Read 15, Robdigphot 27.

Cover photograph: Corbis (Reuters/Richard Chung)

Manufactured in China
CPSIA Compliance Information: Batch #WAW0102PK: For Further Information
contact Rosen Publishing, New York, New York at 1-800-237-9932

Contents

WITHDRAWN

What is rain?

Rain is made up of water droplets that fall from clouds. It is part of the weather. Weather describes the conditions outside at a particular time, for example, whether it is sunny or windy.

All living things on Earth need water to live. Plants live by taking in water through their roots and leaves. People and animals cannot live without water to drink. People also use water for washing and to water crops.

Too little rain makes it very hard to grow crops to eat.

Rain is important for all life, but too much rain can cause floods. A flood is a large amount of water covering an area that is usually dry. Floods can cause a lot of damage. They can destroy houses and roads, and they can kill plants, animals, and people.

Rain fills rivers and lakes with water for animals to drink.

A rainy world

Rain can fall anywhere on Earth. The amount of rain varies in different countries and at different times of year.

Some places, such as **tropical rain forests** in Asia, Africa, and Central and South America, receive a lot of rain. About 10 feet (3 meters) of rain falls on the Amazon rain forest in South America each year. Some places get very little rain, such as the Atacama Desert in Chile. Only 0.04 inch (1 millimeter) of rain falls here each year.

By wearing waterproof clothing, people can still manage to continue with everyday life in heavy rain.

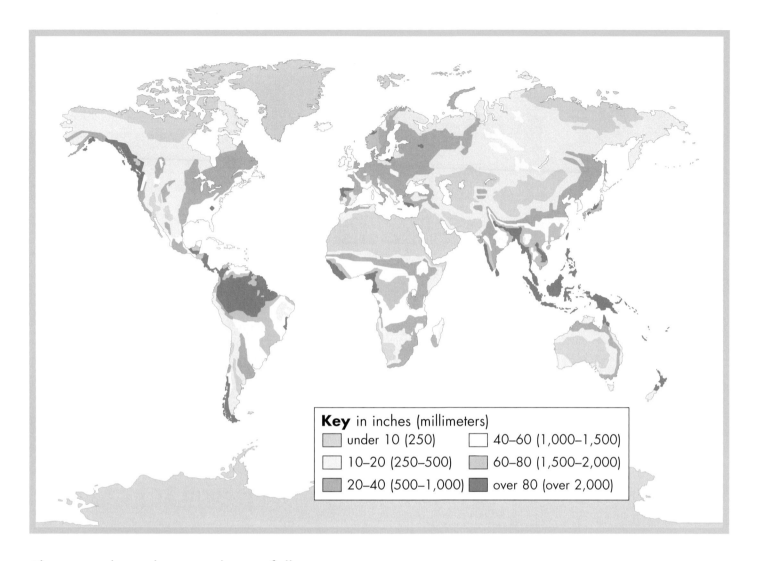

Key in inches (millimeters)
- under 10 (250)
- 10–20 (250–500)
- 20–40 (500–1,000)
- 40–60 (1,000–1,500)
- 60–80 (1,500–2,000)
- over 80 (over 2,000)

This map shows how much rain falls each year in different parts of the world.

In parts of Asia, such as Pakistan and India, **monsoons** bring very heavy rainfall during the summer months. People there look forward to the monsoon, because the rain helps their crops to grow.

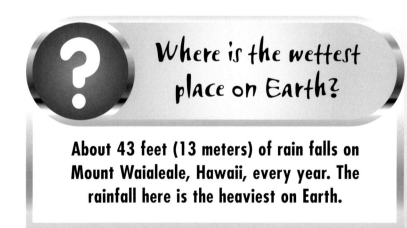

? Where is the wettest place on Earth?

About 43 feet (13 meters) of rain falls on Mount Waialeale, Hawaii, every year. The rainfall here is the heaviest on Earth.

7

The water cycle

Seventy percent of the Earth's surface is covered by water. This water is constantly **recycled**, through a process called the water cycle. In the water cycle, water travels from the Earth's surface to the air, and back to the Earth again. Rain is part of this process.

The Sun's heat warms up the water held in oceans, rivers, and lakes, and on the ground. Some of this water **evaporates** and rises into the air in the form of a gas called water vapor.

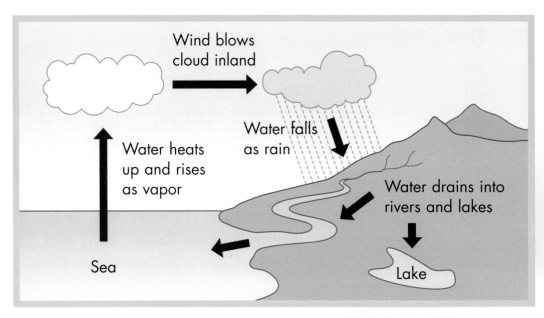

The water cycle has existed ever since water first appeared on Earth, about 3 billion years ago.

The cold air high in the sky makes water vapor cool down and **condense**. It turns the water vapor back into droplets of water. These droplets join together to form clouds. The clouds then produce **precipitation**, which falls back to the ground. Rain is the main type of precipitation.

Most precipitation falls into the oceans, and the rest falls on land. Most of the water that falls on the land eventually flows downhill, back into the ocean.

Most of the water that covers Earth's surface is found in oceans, rivers, and lakes.

9

Will it rain?

People can tell if it is going to rain by looking at the clouds. Five of the main rain clouds to look out for are cirrostratus, altocumulus, stratus, nimbostratus, and cumulonimbus clouds.

Cirrostratus clouds are thin, flat clouds that usually cover the whole sky. They appear about 12–24 hours before it rains.

Altocumulus clouds are big, fluffy gray-white clouds. If these clouds are seen, a thunderstorm may be on its way.

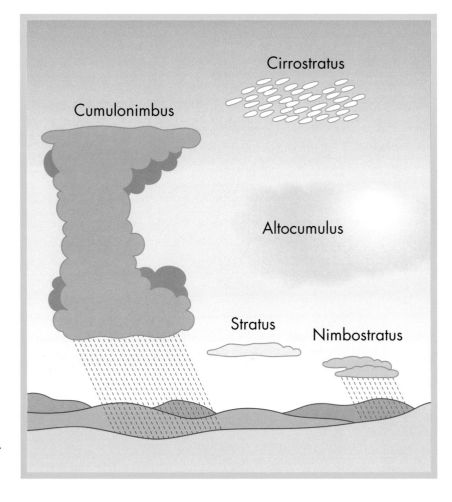

These five clouds are a sign that rain is on its way.

Stratus clouds look like light gray sheets of cloud. They often bring light rain, called drizzle.

Nimbostratus clouds are similar to stratus clouds, but they are a much darker gray. Long, steady rain often falls when these clouds are seen.

Huge, thick, dark-gray clouds, called cumulonimbus clouds, bring heavy rain. These clouds are so dark because they are full of water.

Do meteorologists use clouds to tell the weather?

Meteorologists look at photographs of clouds taken by **satellites** in space. These photographs show where in the world clouds are forming. Meteorologists can then predict where rain may fall, and whether it will be heavy or light.

People without an umbrella quickly get soaked if they are caught in rainfall from cumulonimbus clouds.

Living with rain

People who live in rainy areas have to be prepared for wet weather. They still go to school and work when it rains.

People wear special clothes to keep them dry in the rain. In light rain, people may wear a waterproof jacket and carry an umbrella. In heavy rain, waterproof coats, hats, and boots may be worn.

Rain boots keep people's feet dry even in heavy rainfall.

Some people have jobs related to rainy weather. People who work for environment agencies can tell when a flood may happen. This helps people to stay safe. Police and firefighters clear up after a flood. Water may need to be removed from roads, and buildings may need to be repaired.

People still travel to school and work by bus, trolley car, train, or car during times of heavy rain.

? How are clothes made rainproof?

Rainproof clothes are often made from Gore-Tex. This material is covered in tiny holes. The holes are smaller than water droplets, so rain cannot pass through them. Air can still pass through the holes, however, which keeps people cool.

Living without rain

People, animals, and plants all need rain to live. A long period of time with very little rain is called a drought. If the drought lasts too long, crops, animals, and people may die.

Some parts of Africa are badly affected by drought. Here, people may have to walk for miles to find water, which they then carry home. In dry areas, people also do whatever they can to find and store water. They dig wells to try to find any water that may be underground.

In dry areas, people collect rainwater in tanks, and use it sparingly.

Some animals have adapted to the dry places in which they live. For instance, camels carry huge stores of fat in their humps. This allows them to survive for two weeks without water or food. Plants in dry countries have also adapted to survive. Many have long roots to reach deep into the ground for water.

Many people need their animals for milk and food. If the animals die during a drought, it can be very hard for people to survive, too.

Unbelievable!

Kangaroo rats hop like kangaroos. They can survive without drinking any water at all. They pass very little water in their urine, they never sweat, and they get all the water they need from food.

Is rain useful?

People would not survive without rain. Rain is the main source of all the water used for drinking, cooking, washing, and cleaning.

Because rain is so important, it is collected in **reservoirs**, which are natural or artificial lakes. People then take the water they need from those places. Crops such as coffee and rice cannot grow without large amounts of rain. In Bangladesh and China, rice is grown in large fields that are flooded with water. These are called paddy fields.

Rice grows under water. It is a very important crop in Asia, where it is often eaten daily.

Trees in tropical rain forests, such as the Amazon rain forest, need a lot of rain. The world needs these rainy rain forests. They take in harmful gases, such as carbon dioxide (CO_2), that cause **global warming**. If the Earth warms up too much, its weather could change dramatically. By taking in harmful gases, the rain forests help to control the weather.

More than half of the world's plants and animals, such as this tree frog, live in tropical rain forests.

Unbelievable!

The trees and plants in rain forests make up to 75 percent of the rain they need! Much of the rainwater the trees take in is passed back into the air through their leaves. The water joins the water cycle once more, and falls again as rain.

What is a flood?

A flood occurs when a lot of rain falls in a short time. Rivers and streams cannot contain the extra water, so it overflows onto the land around them.

If there has been a lot of rain, the ground may become full of water. It cannot soak up any more rain. The water then pours back into the rivers and streams, causing more flooding.

Hard surfaces, such as roads, cannot soak up overflowing river water.

When the rain stops, flood water gradually soaks into the fields of a **floodplain**.

 What is a floodplain?

Fields next to a river are often left empty. They are not used for building or farming. Instead, they take up water that has flooded from the river, and stop it reaching nearby buildings. These areas are called floodplains.

Floods can also occur when the weather has been very dry. If it then suddenly rains heavily, the land may be too dry and hard to soak up all the water. The rainwater then builds up on the surface and causes a flood.

Dangerous floods

Floods can cover large areas of land for days or weeks. In extreme floods, water flows down rivers very quickly and violently. If the river cannot hold the water, flooding can suddenly happen. This is called a flash flood and can be dangerous.

Floods can wipe out crops. Flood water can sweep people away, or trap them in their cars. They can destroy people's homes and other buildings. People and animals can drown in the flood water.

A flood flattened and destroyed this corn crop in the Midwest.

Each year in the United States (U.S.A.), more people die as a result of flash floods than from **hurricanes**, lightning, or **tornadoes**. In May 2007, a three-year-long drought in Texas came to an end. Everyone welcomed the rain. But the rain did not stop. It rained constantly for 45 days, causing huge damage to buildings and killing 13 people.

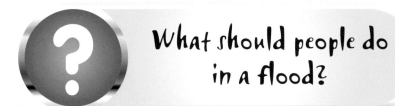

? What should people do in a flood?

People should call the **emergency services** if their home is flooded. They should then wait upstairs for help, as far from the water as possible. People should never go out in a flood. Just 6 inches (15 cm) of fast-moving water can knock a person down.

Rescue workers had to airlift this man from flood waters when Hurricane Katrina hit New Orleans in 2007.

21

What is a monsoon?

A monsoon is a period of very heavy rainfall. Monsoons only happen in some parts of the world, and at certain times of the year. They normally happen when the **season** changes.

Monsoons usually take place over the summer. During a monsoon, a country may receive most of its yearly rainfall. Monsoons normally bring thunderstorms and lightning, too.

The word monsoon comes from the Arabic word mausim, *which means "season."*

Monsoons can last for several months. The monsoons in India and Bangladesh usually start in June and end in September. Smaller monsoons occur at different times in parts of Africa, Australia, and the United States.

Monsoon rainfall can be so heavy that it causes severe floods over large areas of land.

What causes monsoons?

In the summer, the air over the land is warmer than the air over the sea. The warmer air over the land rises into the sky. The cooler air rushes in from the sea to replace it. The cooler air contains lots of **moisture**, and brings the monsoon rain.

23

Living with monsoons

People who live in monsoon zones often rely on the monsoon rain to grow their crops. However, they also have to cope with the heavy monsoon rainfall.

Often, the best way to get around during a monsoon is by bicycle or on foot. Many people also travel by boat when the water rises high. For much of the time, people still manage to travel to school and work during the monsoon season.

When a monsoon causes severe flooding, the only way to travel may be by boat.

Unbelievable!

In 1861, more than 30 feet (9 meters) of rain fell in a single month in Cherrapunji, India!

Monsoons can be dangerous. They sometimes cause floods and **landslides**. These can damage buildings, roads, bridges, and railroad lines. People stay inside as much as they can if flooding occurs. In some countries, such as Vietnam and Bangladesh, people build their houses on **stilts**, to protect them from monsoon floods.

Houses built on stilts keep them high above rainwater that builds up on the ground.

25

Clearing up

After a flood or monsoon, people have to work hard to bring life back to normal. A lot of mess may be left behind, and clearing up can take a long time.

People's houses and everything they own may be ruined. Houses need to be cleaned and repaired. Special fans are used to dry houses completely, so that they do not start to rot. Waterlogged carpets and damaged furniture need to be replaced. Experts must check electrical systems and water supplies, to make sure that they are safe to use.

It can take months for people to clean up their homes after a flood.

Roads may need to be cleared and repaired, and any objects left behind by the flood must be removed. Farmers need to clear away any ruined crops. Then they have to plant new crops.

? Can people be protected from a flood or monsoon?

Warning systems can tell people when a flood or monsoon is coming. This gives them time to move to a safe place. Flood plains can protect towns and villages from flooding. **Flood barriers** can be built to protect people, too.

Roads may be blocked by overturned cars and other heavy objects washed away by a flood.

Make a water cycle

You learned about the water cycle on pages 8 and 9. Now make your own water cycle in this simple experiment.

pages 8 and 9

You will need:
- ruler
- large bowl
- water
- plastic cup
- jug
- plastic wrap
- large rubber band
- small weight

1. Use a ruler to measure 1 inch (2.5 cm) in height on a plastic cup. Pour water into the cup until it reaches the mark.

2. Pour the water from your plastic cup into the bowl.

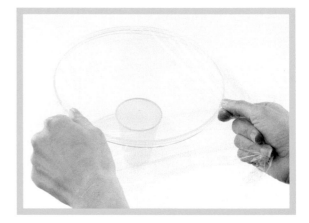

3. Now stand the empty plastic cup the right way up inside the bowl of water.

4. Stretch a sheet of plastic wrap over the top of the bowl.

5. Put a rubber band around the top of the bowl to hold the plastic wrap in place.

6. Place the small weight in the center of the plastic wrap, so that the plastic wrap dips down a little.

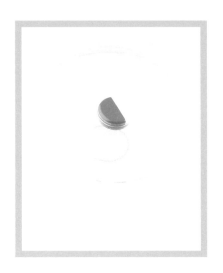

7. Place the bowl outside in sunlight. Leave it there for two to three days.

8. Occasionally return to the bowl over the next few days to see what happens. You should see that droplets of water collect on the underside of the plastic wrap inside the bowl. You should also see water inside the plastic cup.

Understanding your findings

A water cycle was created in your bowl in the following way:

1. Warmth from the sunlight turned the water in the bowl into water vapor. The water vapor rose to the top of the bowl.

2. The water vapor then cooled, and turned into water droplets.

These are the droplets you can see on the underside of the plastic wrap.

3. The weight pushed down the plastic wrap slightly in the center. This made the droplets run down the underside of the plastic wrap. They fell into the cup, just as rain falls from clouds.

29

Glossary

condense change from a gas to a liquid

emergency services organizations that deal with emergencies, such as the police and fire department

evaporate change from a liquid to a gas

flood barrier wall that holds back flood water

flood plain land near a river that often floods

global warming heating up of Earth's temperature

hurricane storm with very strong winds and heavy rain

landslide when large amounts of mud and rocks move quickly down a steep slope

moisture liquid in the form of tiny droplets in the air

monsoon period of extremely heavy rainfall that occurs in some parts of the world each year

precipitation water that falls from clouds, such as rain

recycled when something is used again and again

reservoir man-made or natural lake used for storing water

satellite machine that travels around the Earth in space, and which sends back information about the planet

season one of the four periods of the year: spring, summer, fall, and winter

stilt long piece of wood or metal that holds up a building

tornado spinning funnel of very strong wind

tropical rain forest forest in an area near the part of the world called the tropics, which receives lots of rain

Further Information and Web Sites

Books

Cycles in Nature: The Water Cycle
by Theresa Greenaway (Raintree, 2000)

Earth's Weather and Climate
by Jim Pipe (Gareth Stevens Publishing, 2008)

Inside Fires and Floods
by Nicola Barber (Gareth Stevens Publishing, 2006)

Web Sites

Due to the changing nature of Internet links, PowerKids Press has developed an online list of Web sites related to the subject of this book. This site is updated regularly. Please use this link to access this list:
http://www.powerkidslinks.com/wwise/rain/

Index